HAPPY
THE HIGH-TECH SNOWMAN

A ONE ACT MUSICAL

BY JILL AND MICHAEL GALLINA

TRACK LISTING DEFINITIONS

 This symbol indicates a track number on the CD for the listening version of the song (includes vocals).

 This symbol indicates a track number on the CD for the accompaniment version of the song (instruments only).

ISBN: 978-1-4584-2075-6

Shawnee Press

EXCLUSIVELY DISTRIBUTED BY

 HAL•LEONARD®
CORPORATION

7777 W. BLUEMOUND RD. P.O. BOX 13819 MILWAUKEE, WI 53213

Visit Shawnee Press online at www.shawneepress.com
Visit Hal Leonard online at www.halleonard.com

INTRODUCTION

With school closed for snow, a group of friends look forward to an afternoon at Samantha's house. Surrounded by their electronic devices, the children bury themselves in a flurry of individual hi-tech activities. Surprised by the children's reluctance to go outdoors, Samantha's Mom suggests that they build a snowman. Unimpressed with what they think is a somewhat dated activity, the children reluctantly leave the house. Once outdoors, they find themselves face to face with a walking, talking snowman named Happy. He tells them that he has come to life to learn more about the current wave of technology.

Happy soon gets lost in a blizzard of techno-speak and a world of devices that both astound and confuse him. When one of his new friends posts a video on YouTube of Happy dancing, his life takes a dramatic turn. The posting goes viral and scientists, reporters, and paparazzi all want to track him down. This triggers a turn of events that causes his young friends to set in motion a "flash mob" that ends in rescuing Happy from his pursuers. Six songs, a clever script, and memorable characters provide the basis for this timely, fun-filled, and upbeat musical.

Beginning in late fall and extending throughout the winter months, *Happy, the High-Tech Snowman* will prove to be a production that receives kudos and applause from both students and parents. Given its nondenominational orientation toward the winter season, it lends itself to a number of community and instructional settings.

CONTENTS
Scenes and Musical Numbers

Performance time: approx. 35 minutes

CAST OF CHARACTERS

Happy the Snowman
Samantha
Mom (Samantha's Mom, Mrs. Jones)
Dad (Samantha's Dad, Mr. Jones)
TV News Anchor #1
TV News Anchor #2
TV News Camera Person (non-speaking part)
Paparazzi #1
Paparazzi #2 (2–8 paparazzi as permitted by performance area)
Three Professors:
      Dr. Sigmund Floyd, Psychologist
      Dr. Hail Storm, Meteorologist
      Dr. Hugh Mankind, Anthropologist
Randy, Kim, Dan, Katie, Woody, Janet, Mike, Sheryl (Samantha's friends)
(additional friends with non-speaking parts may be added)

COSTUMES

For indoor scenes children and parents are dressed in casual clothes. During outdoor scenes, all cast members wear coats and winter outerwear such as hats, scarves, and mittens.

Happy the Snowman's costume can be as simple or elaborate as time and talent allow. A simple snowman look can be created by wearing a white long-sleeved tee shirt, white slacks, black top hat, black mittens, and black sunglasses. Black self-stick felt may be used to cut out 3 buttons that can adhere to the front of the tee shirt. We highly recommend this simple approach to the costumes, as several children in the last scene dress as "Happy" look-alike snowmen. Another option is using white fleece warm-up suits turned inside out to create a fuzzy look. A third would be to purchase inexpensive white paper doctor scrubs available at party stores. All of the snowmen have sunglasses and a top hat. Inexpensive top hats can also be purchased at party stores.

The news anchors should be dressed in business attire (sports jackets or dresses) and the scientists can wear wacky clothes and wild, colorful wigs, to look wild and crazy.

SET SUGGESTIONS

This musical requires three sets: living room, TV studio, and outdoor scene. In order to simplify set requirements, the living room and the TV studio appear on stage right and the outdoor scene is on stage left. The outdoor scene occupies 2/3 of the performance area and the living room/TV studio occupies the remaining 1/3.

It is suggested that the living room/TV studio be composed of two flats (two walls) that are formed into an L-shape. The outdoor scene consists of a snowy landscape set to stage left of the indoor scenes. While a working door can be built into the flat on the side of the outdoor scene, it is not necessary. Entrances and exits from the indoors to the outdoors and vice-versa can be made without an actual door.

The only set changes that take place occur during an outdoor scene with the living room is changed into the TV studio and during another outdoor scene with the TV studio is changed back into the living room.

SET PROPS

The following set props are required. As time and resources permit, you can add as much detail to the scenes as you see fit.

Living Room:
a. A window (snowing outside) is attached to the flat with Velcro (replaced with a TV channel logo).
b. Two chairs, one end table, floor lamp, and if possible a light-weight love seat/couch, two to three large pillows for the floor.

TV Studio:
a. A desk for the two news anchors.
b. TV channel logo is attached with Velcro (replacing the window).
c. Three chairs for the scientists.

Outdoor Snow Scene:
a. An evergreen tree large enough for Happy to stand behind. Can be either an artificial Christmas tree or a free-standing cutout of a tree.
b. If possible, include other trees in this scene.

HAND PROPS

Scene I
>   Coffee cup
>   Newspaper
>   Electronics (cardboard cutouts painted black can be used to represent the actual items) — 8 cell phones, 2 game pads, 2 hand-held games, 3 laptops.

Scene II
>   Same as Scene I.

Scene III
>   Sunglasses (for Happy)
>   Ten cell phones

Scene IV
>   Flash cameras for the paparazzi (photojournalists).

Scene V
>   One cell phone
>   One game pad

Scene VI
>   Four cell phones

Scene VII
>   Video camera (real or made from a shoe box with a cardboard tub for a lens)
>   Flash cameras for paparazzi
>   One cell phone

While not essential, a prerecorded cell phone ring and text message chime can be useful as a sound effect for some of the scenes.

STAGING AND CHOREOGRAPHY SUGGESTIONS

Song 1: Might as Well Put on a Show
The characters should be standing in tableau form on either side of the performance area. As each different group or character is sung about in the lyrics, have them step forward and do a sweeping bow to the audience and then step back into place and remain in tableau form.

Song 2: Make No Apology for Technology
During the "rap" section of the song, have "rap soloists" improvise motions and movement that coordinate with the lyrics. During the chorus melody part, have children hold up items such as laptops, game pads, cell phones, etc. and sway them over their heads in time to the music.

Song 3: Something Is Wrong with This Picture
For a really interesting effect, take pictures of your cast members or have them bring pictures from home of them at their computers, texting, playing on their game pad, or doing something that involves technology, but they must be alone in the picture. During the singing of the song, project these pictures on an overhead screen to be viewed by the audience.

Song 4: Text Talk
During the song when children are supposed to be teaching Happy to text, they should pantomime texting the letters on their cell phones. Happy will need a cell phone to do the same. On the chorus, they sway back and forth. On the lyrics beginning with "your fingers do the talking," have them work their fingers with hands out front as if playing the keys on a piano. On the lyrics "Don't have to say a thing," after the word 'thing' they can do the "lips sealed" motion by holding their thumb and index finger together and swiping them across their lips.

Song 5: Gotta Find Our Man!
This is a comedic chase song where the three scientists are frantically searching for Happy. They run through the audience and search behind and under seats and any other comedic areas that are appropriate. During the song, members of the media enter snapping photos and join in the search. For added comedy you may choose to have a few students dressed as police officers joining in as well, blowing police whistles, etc.

Song 6: Gotta Find Our Man! (Reprise)
This instrumental reprise has a few vocal lines that are optional. It is the flash mob scene when all the children appear disguised as Happy in snowman outfits. It should be a confusing frenetic scene as the children are trying to be a distraction and lead the scientists and media astray.

Song 7: Get Happy!
Choreography suggestions:
Measures 1–4: Sway from side to side, left to right, on beats 1 and 3.
Measure 5: Snap fingers on beats 2 and 4.
Measure 6: Clap hands on beats 2 and 4.
Measures 7–8: Strut around with hands moving up and down close to sides in moves like a wooden soldier.
Measures 9–12: Fingers spread, hands frame both sides of face. Sway left to right two times per measure on beats 1 and 3.
Repeat:
Measure 5: Clap hands on beats 2 and 4.
Measure 6: Tap toes on beats 2 and 4.
Measures 7–8: Improvise wild and crazy moves.
Measures 9, 13, 14: Fingers spread, hands frame both sides of face. Sway left to right two times per measure on beats 1 and 3.
Measure 15: Shrug shoulders, flip hands to each side in question pose.
Measures 16–23: Sway left to right on beats 1 and 3.
Measure 24: Snap fingers on beats 2 and 4.
Measure 25: Clap hands on beats 2 and 4.

Measures 26–27: Using index fingers on both sides of mouth, make an arc to show a smile and hold.

Measures 28–31: Fingers spread, hands frame both sides of face and sway left to right two times per measure on beats 1 and 3.

Measures 32–39: Follow motions as directed in lyrics.

Measures 40–41: Using index fingers on both sides of mouth, make an arc to show a smile and hold.

Measures 42–43: Holding smile, sway left to right two times per measure on beats 1 and 3.

Measure 44: Snap fingers on beats 2 and 4.

Measure 45: Clap hands on beats 2 and 4.

Measures 46–47: Using index fingers on both sides of mouth, make an arc to show a smile and hold.

Measures 48–49: One-third of students singing: fingers spread, hands frame both sides of face and sway left to right two times per measure on beats 1 and 3. The other two-thirds of singers are frozen in place for these two measures.

Measures 50–51: Students who were just singing point to a third of the other students who have been frozen in place and they then join in singing, fingers spread, hands frame both sides of face and sway left to right two times per measure on beats 1 and 3. The last third of singers are still frozen in place for these two measures.

Measures 52–53: Students who were just singing point to the last group of students who have been frozen in place and then all join in fingers spread, hands frame both sides of face and sway left to right two times per measure on beats 1 and 3.

Measures 54–55: Hand outstretched, point toward audience.

Measures 56–57: Fingers spread, hands frame both sides of face and sway from left to right two times per measure on beats 1 and 3.

Measure 58: Sunburst.

Measure 59: Freeze in place.

Song 7: Get Happy! (Reprise)

During the reprise of the song, some of the cast may run into the audience and encourage the audience members to stand up and clap, snap, tap, and dance, etc., with the performers.

1. MIGHT AS WELL PUT ON A SHOW
Chorus

by MICHAEL *and* JILL GALLINA

Continuing the Tradition of Shawnee Press Excellence

and when you meet them we're sure__ you'll a - gree. Throw in some

me, and when you meet them we're sure__ you'll a - gree. Throw in some

T - V types__ that are full of hype,__ add some wild and cra - zy sci - en - tists, too.__

T - V types__ that are full of hype,__

Sounds like the mak - ings of a real - ly good show,__ but with a

Sounds like the mak - ings of a real - ly good show,__ but with a

snow-man we bet - ter add snow! Well, danc - ing bears___ we
Rab - bits pulled___ from

have - n't got_____ but we'll make up for it with
mag - ic hats_____ well, we're real sor - ry but we

twists in the plot! And now they've learned their parts_____ and they
have none of that! But they've all learned their parts_____ and they

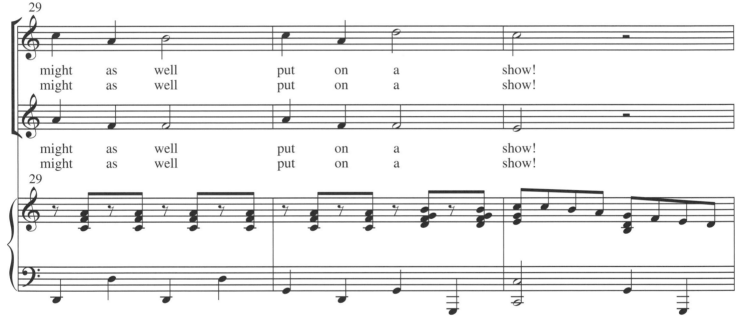

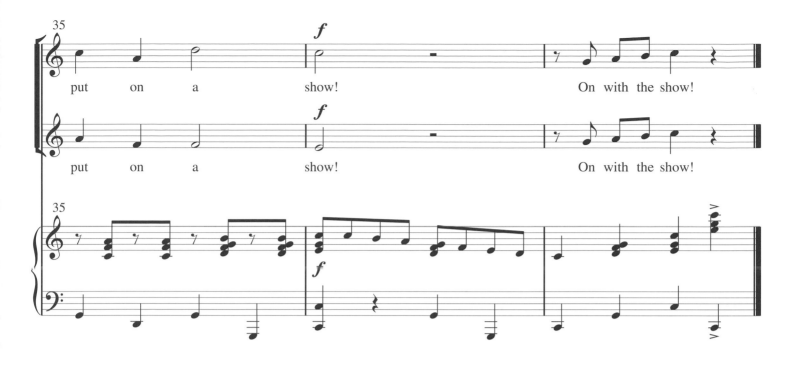

put on a show! On with the show!

put on a show! On with the show!

Scene I

The scene opens on Samantha's living room. (Lights are off on the outdoor scene. Mom enters stage left and walks toward stage right while calling out to Samantha.

MOM: *(carrying a coffee cup, sits down to read the newspaper after speaking)* Samantha, don't bother to rush. We just got the call; school's closed. This snowstorm's a real problem.

SAMANTHA: *(enters stage right)* Problem? Come on, Mom, it's our first snow day. All the kids will be really psyched.

Dad enters stage left while Mom is speaking.

MOM: Well, I can understand that. You're all looking forward to playing in the snow; sledding, snow forts, and making a snowman.

SAMANTHA: *(plops into a chair while speaking)* Mom, get real. My friends aren't into that kind of stuff.

DAD: *(looks toward Mom)* I just checked on the train schedule. Nothing's moving. It looks like we're not going to work. Samantha, what about you? Got plans for today?

SAMANTHA: Dad, please, *(slight pause)* plans? All the kids are gonna just hang out.

Lights are turned on in the outdoor scene. As Samantha is speaking, her friends walk through the outdoor scene toward the living room. They pantomime speaking to each other. A knock or doorbell is heard. Mom and Dad look at each other as if to say "who can that be?"

HAPPY, THE HIGH-TECH SNOWMAN – Teacher Edition

SAMANTHA: *(continues speaking)* Oh, I forgot. *(a knock/bell is heard again)* I sent out a Tweet inviting all of the kids over.

Mom gets up and walks toward stage left to let Samantha's friends in the house.

DAD: Tweet? You mean you just have to tweet and the whole flock comes over to roost!

SAMANTHA: Come on, Dad. *(Samantha gets up to greet her friends.)*

Samantha's friends enter from stage left. As they make their noisy entrance, they are joking and laughing. They take off their coats, throw them in a pile, and begin to announce what they have brought.

MIKE: We brought a whole pile of goodies.

MOM: Mike, you didn't have to. We have plenty of ...

SAMANTHA: *(interrupting)* Mom! He doesn't mean food.

Mom silently puts her hand to her mouth as if to say "oops."

RANDY: Kim and I brought our new game pads.

DAN: Got my new cell phone.

KATIE: Woody and I brought our hand-held games.

JANET: Mike and I have our laptops.

SHERYL: Hope your internet connection can handle it. I plan to stream movies.

DAD: *(speaking slowly and incredulously)* I don't get it! *(pauses, and shakes his head in disbelief)* Why bother getting together if you're all gonna do your own thing?

SAMANTHA: Dad, do you have to?

WOODY: *(speaking like a rapper)* Mr. Jones, we are the future. We're not apologizin' for technolo-gizin'.

All the kids nod their heads in approval. Mom and Dad raise their hands as if to say "Oh, well!" and exit stage right.

2. MAKE NO APOLOGY
FOR TECHNOLOGY
Kids

by MICHAEL *and* JILL GALLINA

Continuing the Tradition of Shawnee Press Excellence

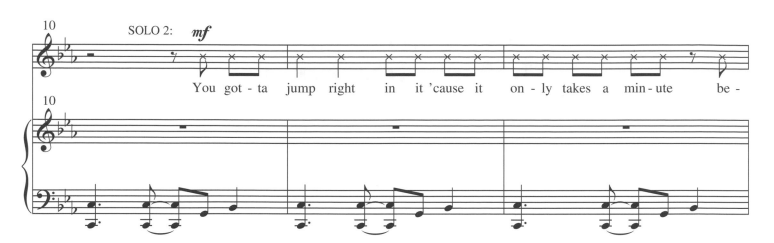

SOLO 2: *mf*

You got-ta jump right in it 'cause it on-ly takes a min-ute be-

ALL: *mf*   **15**

fore what's new is old, that's right! Make no a-pol-o-gy___ for tech-

nol-o-gy,___ so you bet-ter make up your mind. Are you

in the game?___ If not, it's a shame___ 'cause you're gon-na be left be-hind!

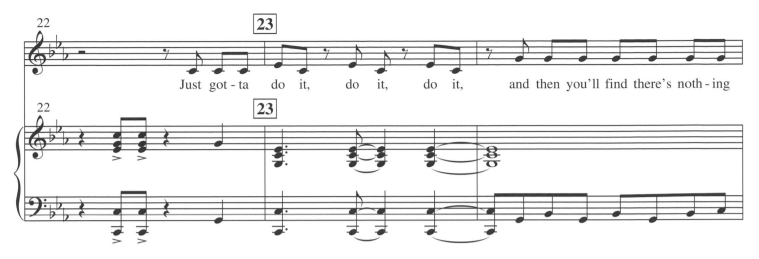

Just got-ta do it, do it, do it, and then you'll find there's noth-ing

to it, to it, to it. Just got-ta do it, do it, do it,

SOLO 3: *mf*

and then you'll find there's noth-ing to it, to it, to it. So come on,

girls and boys, it's time to make some noise. Folks, lis-ten up to what we say.

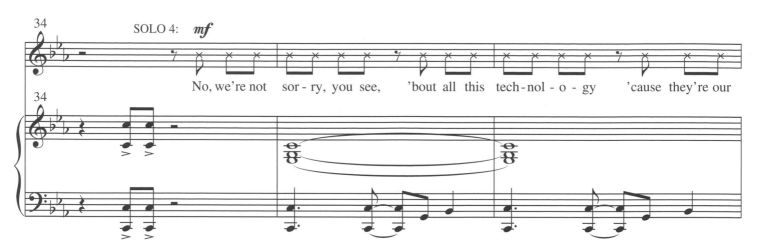

No, we're not sor - ry, you see, 'bout all this tech - nol - o - gy 'cause they're our

new toys of to - day! That's right! Make no a - pol - o - gy ___ for tech -

nol - o - gy, ___ so you bet - ter make up your mind. Are you

in the game? If not, it's a shame ___ 'cause you're gon - na be left be - hind!

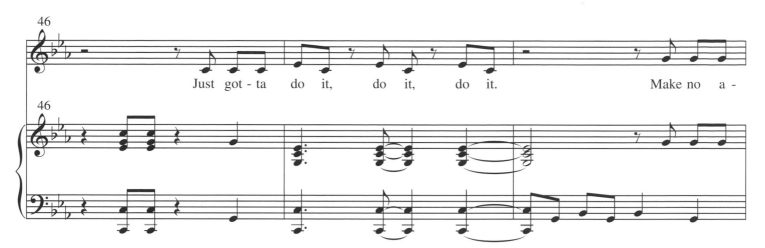

Just got-ta do it, do it, do it. Make no a-

pol-o-gy__ for tech-nol-o-gy,__ so you bet-ter make up your mind.

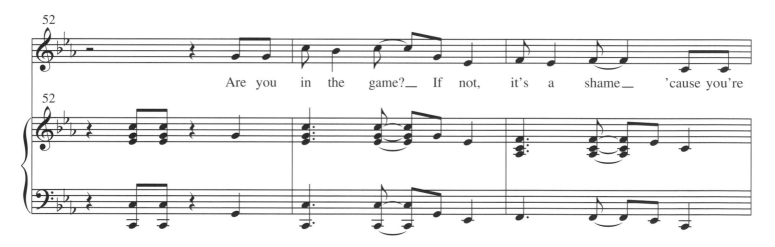

Are you in the game?__ If not, it's a shame__ 'cause you're

gon-na be left be-hind! So you bet-ter make up your mind

At the end of the song, the kids assume a variety of comfortable positions around the room and ad lib: "I'm goin' on YouTube." "Know any good movies?" "I have to text a friend." "Gotta check something on Google," etc. The room starts to become silent as they turn on their various devices.

Scene II

All of the kids are totally immersed in their technodevices and are periodically heard speaking to someone on their cell phone. Kids on game pads periodically give out a "yeah" or "no," but for the most part there is no interaction among them. They are all lost in the electronic world of their personal devices.

Approximately 10–15 seconds pass between the end of Song 2. and Dad's entrance. Dad enters stage left while looking from side to side in disbelief. He begins speaking softly, but gets louder.

DAD: Hi, guys. *(waits a second, looks around, sarcastically)* Hello?? ... Hello???? Is anybody home?

The kids are startled and slowly look up from their devices.

SAMANTHA: What's up, Dad? Is something wrong?

Mom enters from stage right.

DAD: You guys are hanging out together, but you're all doing your own thing. Don't you ever chat with one another?

RANDY: Sure we chat, we just do it on our computers.

MOM: What's the point of having friends over if you barely talk to each other? It's beautiful outside in the snow. Why don't you go outside and play?

SAMANTHA: *(embarrassed)* Come on, Mom! We're not little children.

KATIE: Mrs. Jones, we're practically grown up. Do you really think we should go outside and, and ... *(slight pause)* ... PLAY?

DAD: *(becoming excited)* Why not? When I was a kid, you couldn't keep me indoors.

MOM: Don't get excited, dear. Things are very different today.

DAN: Mr. Jones, we didn't mean to upset you. Things aren't as bad as they seem.

JANET: Dan's right, Mr. Jones. Kids are still kids. It's just that a lot has changed since you were our age.

DAD: You're right!! Things have certainly changed. I'm looking around this room and believe me, something is very wrong with this picture!!

3. SOMETHING IS WRONG WITH THIS PICTURE

Mr. and Mrs. Jones

by MICHAEL *and* JILL GALLINA

Continuing the Tradition of Shawnee Press Excellence

20

get them to stop __ when they're on that lap - top! Some - thing is wrong __ with this
glued to a screen __ with no con - ver - sa - tion. Some - thing is wrong __ with this

pic - ture, can't you see! They're
pic - ture. Woe is me!

1. *(to pg. 19, m. 5)*

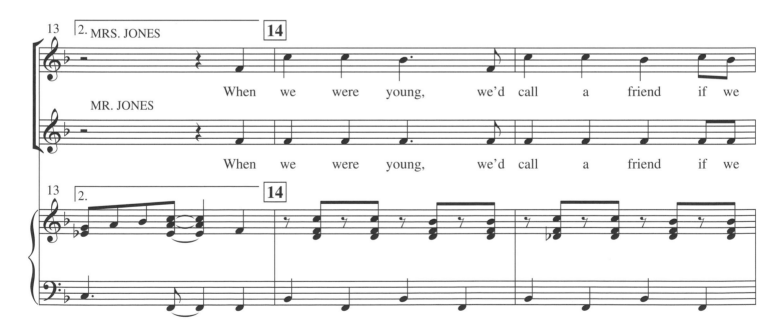

2. MRS. JONES

When we were young, we'd call a friend if we

MR. JONES

When we were young, we'd call a friend if we

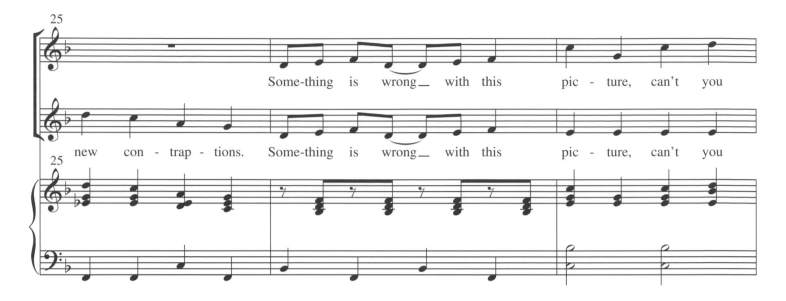

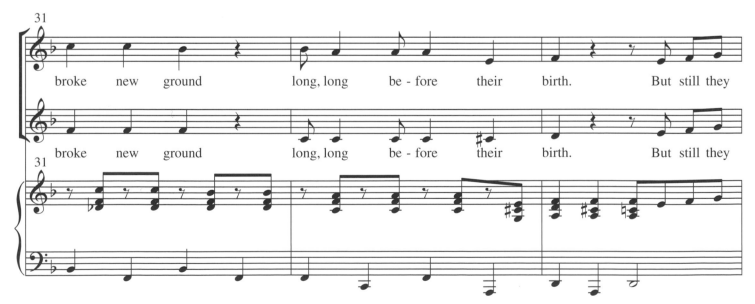

treat us just like rel - ics from a long time a - go____ when

treat us just like rel - ics from a long time a - go____ when

38

di - no - saurs roamed the earth. Be - lieve me! When we were young, we knew

di - no - saurs roamed the earth. Be - lieve me!

how to have fun.__

And we nev - er had one__ of those gui - tar he - roes.

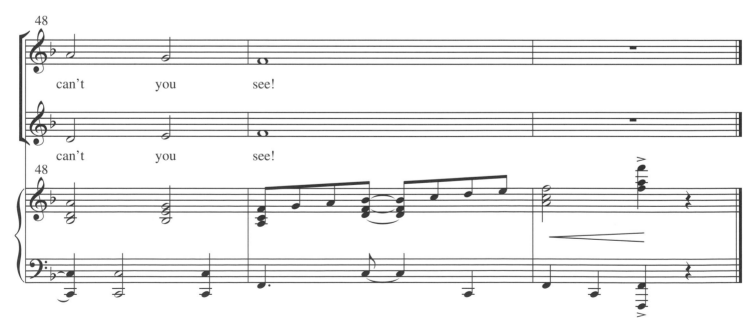

Having tried so hard to get his point across, Dad becomes exhausted and falls into a chair at the very end of the song.

MOM: We realize it's a different world, but some things stay the same—like having fun making a snowman. When I was your age we made a snowman, and he really came to life! After we put on his button eyes and carrot nose he actually began to speak and he ...

SAMANTHA: *(interrupting)* OK, Mom. You don't have to make up crazy stories just to get us to go outdoors. *(slowly and with resignation)* We'll go outside and make a snowman.

ALL THE KIDS: In the cold?

SAMANTHA: *(snapping back at them)* Yes, in the cold.

KIM: Come on, guys; let's get our coats on.

They mumble and grunt as they grudgingly put on their coats and slowly exit to the outdoor scene. When outdoors, they pantomime speaking to each other as they stand around rubbing their hands. They appear to be quite cold and very unhappy.

DAD: *(to Mom)* Congratulations on getting them out of the house. But how did you come up with that unbelievable story?

MOM: Unbelievable? We'll see about that.

Dad shakes his head in disbelief as he and Mom exit stage right. Lights are turned off on the living room portion of the performance area and it is reset for Scene IV, a TV newscast.

Scene III

Before the lights are turned up on the outdoor portion of the performance area, Happy prepares for his entrance by positioning himself behind an evergreen tree that is on stage left in the outdoor scene.

MIKE: Don't stand around like a bunch of frozen popsicles. If you wanna get back inside, we'd better get going.

KIM: Where do we start? I never made a snowman.

SHERYL: I'll look it up on my cell phone.

WOODY: It's not rocket science. Just start rolling three snowballs that get bigger and bigger. You need two for the middle and bottom and a small one for the head.

DAN: Sounds easy enough. What are we waiting for?

RANDY: Sheryl and I will go ask Mrs. Jones for buttons and sunglasses for his eyes. *(Both exit stage right behind the indoor scene.)*

KATIE: I think the snow's deeper in the backyard. Let's start there and roll the snow around to the front.

The kids exit stage right behind the indoor scene. When they are gone, Happy steps from behind the evergreen tree and stands in front of it. Randy and Sheryl return and are amazed to see a snowman.

SHERYL: (with sunglasses in hand) Look! It's a snowman! How'd they do that? (points to the snowman) He's even wearing a top hat.

RANDY: (loudly calling out) Hey, guys! Come on back! How'd you make the snowman so soon?

Woody leads the kids on as they enter from stage right.

WOODY: What do you mean? (looks in amazement and points at Happy) What? Where did he come from?

The kids gather on each side of Happy.

SAMANTHA: (speaking slowly as if something is really spooky) I think I know. Sheryl, do you have the sunglasses?

SHERYL: (hands the sunglasses to Samantha) Yeah. Here they are.

Samantha stands in front of Happy and puts the sunglasses on him; he then begins to move. The kids step back with a touch of fear and a great deal of amazement.

HAPPY: Hi, kids! My name is Happy.

KIM: Very funny, Mr. Jones. (turns to Samantha) Your father will do anything to get us to stay outside in the snow!

The kids go to Happy and start poking him, tickling him, etc.

JANET: Cool snowsuit! Where did you dig that one up, Mr. Jones? (Kids continue to poke and prod Happy.)

HAPPY: Hey, that's not funny. Stop poking. (he giggles) Even though I might seem cold on the outside, I'm very ticklish! (he giggles again)

KATIE: I don't believe it. I think he IS real!

DAN: (in disbelief) A walking, talking snowman ...

The kids all begin to talk at once, ad libbing "No one will believe this." "This can't be real." "Gimme a break." "No way!", etc.

DAN: C'mon everyone, CHILL!

HAPPY: Chill!! One of my very favorite words!

The kids all laugh and ad lib. "Very funny." "Ha, ha, ha!", etc.)

SAMANTHA: What in the world are you doing here?

HAPPY: Well ... I'm not exactly from this world.

SAMANTHA: That doesn't answer our question. What are you doing here?

HAPPY: Sorry, I tend to drift ... Actually, my friends set up a slush fund to send me here to learn about technology. Where I come from we don't have a clue. You might say we've been frozen out. Can you help?

MIKE: Well, uh, sure. Hmmm, where to begin?? I know, let's start with something easy like cell phones. *(He whips his cell phone out of his pocket.)* They do lots of things, but most of all we love sending text messages. Wanna learn how to do that?

HAPPY: Sounds like fun.

KIM: First you have to learn a new way of spelling. Like, if you wanted to say "laugh out loud," you don't type it all out.

HAPPY: No?

JANET: You just type LOL.

HAPPY: Wow, that's cool! Teach me more.

At one point during the following song, Happy begins to dance. Janet holds up her cell phone and makes a video of him dancing around.

4. TEXT TALK
Happy, Boys, and Girls

by MICHAEL *and* JILL GALLINA

Continuing the Tradition of Shawnee Press Excellence

HAPPY, THE HIGH-TECH SNOWMAN – Teacher Edition

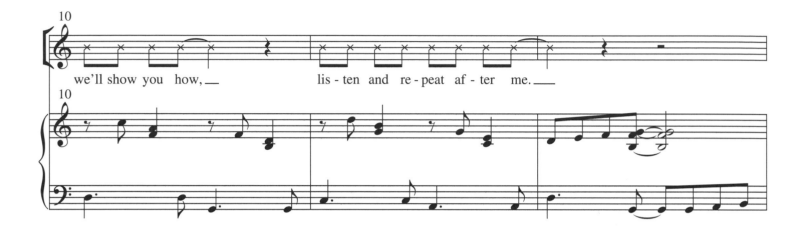

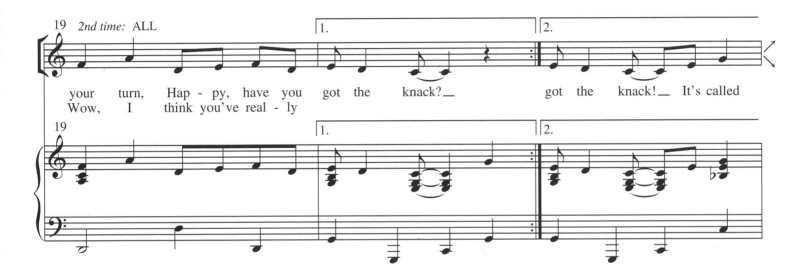

HAPPY, THE HIGH-TECH SNOWMAN – Teacher Edition

let - ters they'll be walk - in', it's text talk, text talk and you

let - ters they'll be walk - in', it's text talk, text talk and you

don't have to say a thing!

don't have to say a thing!

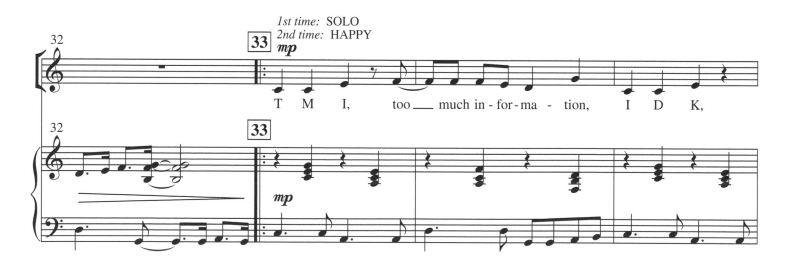

1st time: SOLO
2nd time: HAPPY

T M I, too ___ much in - for - ma - tion, I D K,

I don't know.__ A W__ H F Y, are we hav-ing fun yet?
dou-ble - u

All right, Hap - py, it's your turn to go.__ in the know__ it's called
Wow! I think you're real - ly

text talk, text talk. Just let your fin-gers do the talk-in' cross the
text talk, text talk. Just let your fin-gers do the talk-in' cross the

let - ters they'll be walk- in', it's   text talk,   text   talk   and you

let - ters they'll be walk- in', it's   text talk,   text   talk   and you

don't have to say   a   thing!   Don't have to say   a   thing!

don't have to say   a   thing!   Don't have to say   a   thing!

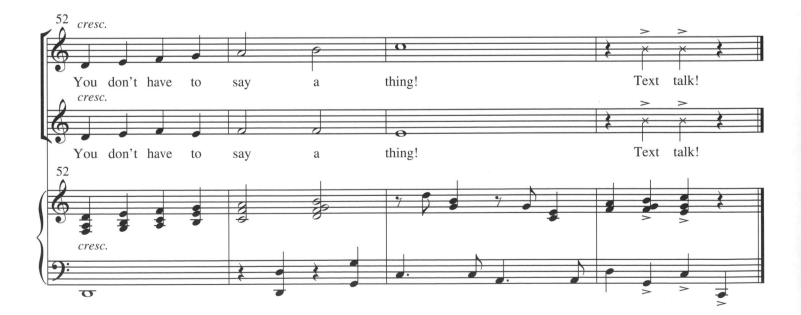

cresc.

You don't have   to   say   a   thing!   Text talk!

cresc.

You don't have   to   say   a   thing!   Text talk!

cresc.

JANET:	While you were singing and dancing, I made a video and I'm gonna post it on YouTube.
HAPPY:	YouTube? That sounds funny. What's that all about?
MIKE:	Come inside with us, Happy. We'll post your video and show you how YouTube works.
HAPPY:	I'm not sure I should go inside.
KATIE:	What's the problem?
HAPPY:	Lend me your cell phone.

Happy takes Katie's phone and texts a message, then hands it back and they all gather around to look.

MIKE:	I-D-W-T-B-A-D, what's that mean?
HAPPY:	It means "I don't want to be a drip!" *(slight pause)* Get it?
KIM:	Very funny! Happy's already making up his own texts. You are really hot stuff!
HAPPY:	*(agitated)* Not hot! Don't ever say the word "hot" in front of a snowman!
RANDY:	Sorry, Happy. How about this? You're cool, real cool!
HAPPY:	*(wipes his brow)* Phew! Cool is much better!

The kids lead Happy off stage right and exit behind the TV news studio.

Scene IV

At the end of the outdoor scene, lights go up on a TV news studio where two news anchors are seated at a small table on stage right and three scientists are seated on stage left.

NEWS ANCHOR #1:	We interrupt this broadcast with an unbelievable story about a singing and dancing snowman. It has just been confirmed that the YouTube video that went viral over the weekend was in fact true.
NEWS ANCHOR #2:	Evidently there really is a walking, talking snowman. We have three experts who have authenticated the video and will tell us how they plan to investigate this matter further.
NEWS ANCHOR #1:	They are well-known scientists who specialize in anthropology, psychology, and meteorology.
NEWS ANCHOR #2:	We welcome our anthropologist, Dr. Hugh *(pause)* Mankind; meteorologist, Dr. Hail Storm, and psychologist, Dr. Sigmund Floyd.

NEWS ANCHOR #1:	Professors, please share with us some of your initial thoughts on this snowman who appears to have come to life.
DR. STORM:	As a meteorologist, I believe that the snowman was created when El Niño gave La Niña the cold shoulder.
DR. MANKIND:	I could not disagree with you more. This snowman creature is a missing link from the early Ice Age.
DR. FLOYD:	Gentlemen, gentlemen, you are both far from the truth. It is quite clear that he has a rare mental condition called frigid personality disorder. It generally happens when you are raised with flaky relatives.
NEWS ANCHOR #2:	While there continues to be disagreement among our experts, questions remain unanswered. *(speaking slowly and with emphasis)* What is he? Who is he and where is he?
DR. STORM:	It's clear we've got to find him and when we do, all of your questions will be answered.
NEWS ANCHOR #1:	If you do find your snowman, what do you plan to do with him?
DR. FLOYD:	First, to make sure he doesn't melt, we'll have to put him in a freezer.
NEWS ANCHOR #2:	That's a chilling thought!
DR. MANKIND:	There's not a minute to waste. We can't wait for a sunny day. We've gotta find him right now!

When the music starts, the three scientists stand and wildly exit into the audience. The news anchors exit stage right. Lights should be turned off in the TV studio and house lights put on. The scientists are madly searching (under chairs, behind curtains, etc.) for Happy as they sing along with the chorus. As they move about, members of the media (paparazzi) join in the search, snapping photos with flash cameras. During the song the TV studio is changed back to Samantha's living room.

5. GOTTA FIND OUR MAN!

Scientists, Media, and Children

by MICHAEL *and* JILL GALLINA

Continuing the Tradition of Shawnee Press Excellence

HAPPY, THE HIGH-TECH SNOWMAN – Teacher Edition

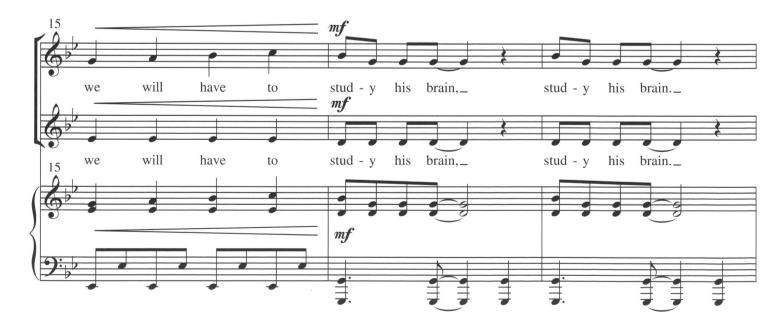

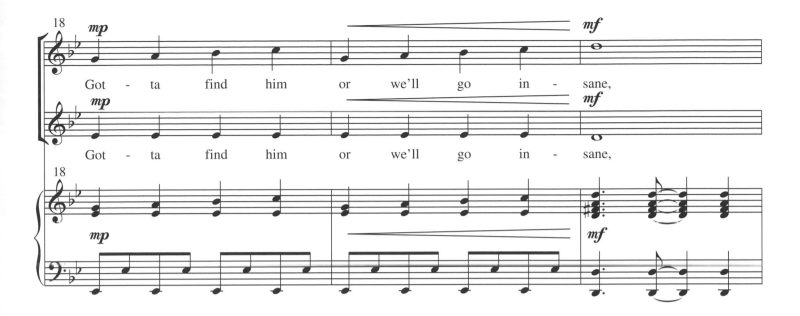

Got - ta find him or we'll go in - sane,

Got - ta find him or we'll go in - sane,

it's gon - na drive us in - sane.___

it's gon - na drive us in - sane.___

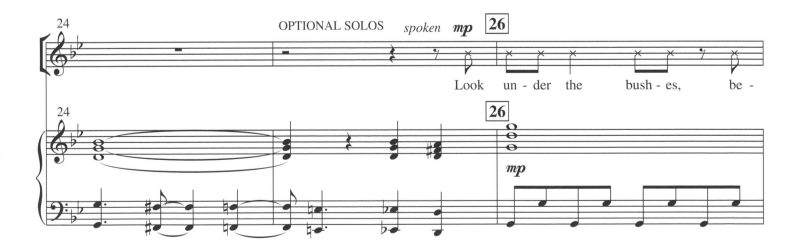

OPTIONAL SOLOS *spoken* **mp** **26**

Look un - der the bush - es, be -

HAPPY, THE HIGH-TECH SNOWMAN – Teacher Edition

38

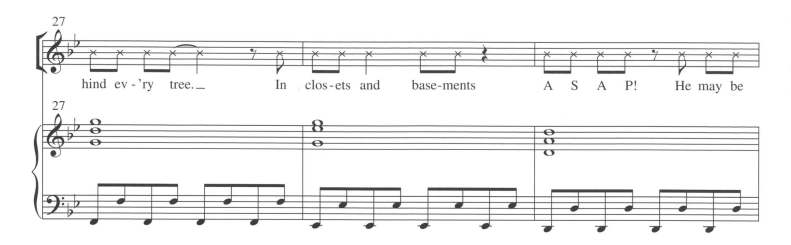

hind ev-'ry tree.__ In clos-ets and base-ments A S A P! He may be

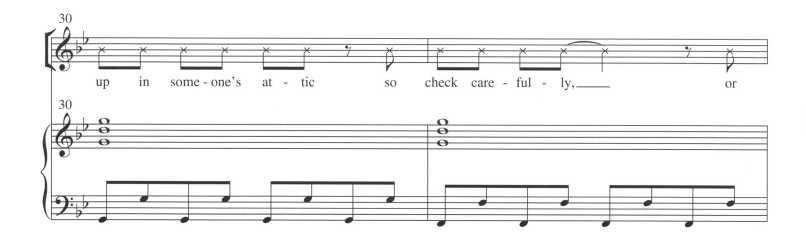

up in some-one's at - tic so check care-ful-ly,___ or

hid - ing in a freez-er's where he just might be!

cresc. *f*

cresc. *f*

HAPPY, THE HIGH-TECH SNOWMAN – Teacher Edition

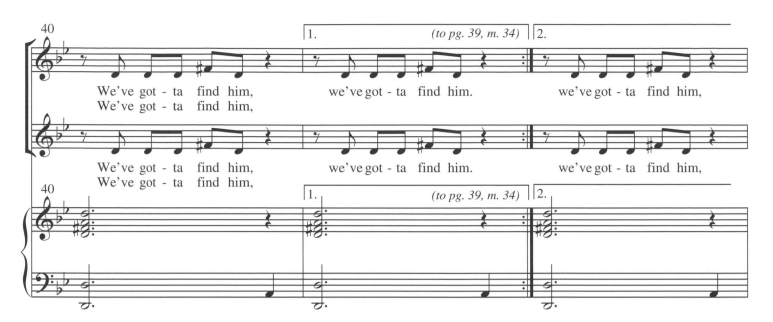

We've got-ta find him, we've got-ta find him. we've got-ta find him,
We've got-ta find him,

and un-til we do, ___ we'll check out ev-'ry clue. ___ It's
and un-til we do, ___ we'll check out ev-'ry clue. ___ It's

up to me and you ___ to find him right now! ___
up to me and you ___ to find him right now! ___

Scene V

At the conclusion of the song, all exit and house lights are turned off. As the lights are turned up on the outdoor scene, Woody and Mike are explaining something to Happy. They are all looking at Woody's cell phone.

HAPPY: *(sadly)* Oh, I don't think I'll ever understand this technology business. I'm really confused.

WOODY: Come on, Happy. It's not that hard.

MIKE: This is how it works. Janet took a video of you with her cell phone and then posted it on YouTube.

HAPPY: Post, what's that mean?

WOODY: Well, it's kinda like putting up a notice that you post, like on a bulletin board.

HAPPY: Oh, I see. So instead of using a thumbtack, you put it up electronically.

MIKE: That's it! I think you've got it. Come on, now, I'll teach you how to play guitar hero!

Dan and Janet run in stage left. They are out of breath and very excited.

JANET: You won't believe it. We've been watching the news and we have a problem.

DAN: The video of Happy went viral and millions of people want to know all about the snowman who came to life.

HAPPY: Viral? Is there a disease going around?

WOODY: Going viral on the internet means that the video we posted of you spread all over and a lot of people have seen it.

JANET: Yeah, and now a whole bunch of people want to get hold of Happy. News people, scientists, paparazzi, and who knows who else?

HAPPY: I don't want to see a lot of people. I only want to be around children who are my friends.

DAN: Don't worry, Happy. We'll figure something out.

MIKE: Better call the other kids. Happy, you hide behind the evergreen tree. We'll get back to you as soon as we can.

As Janet begins to make a call, the lights on the outdoor scene are turned off and the kids exit stage left. Lights come up on Samantha's living room. As the scene opens, Samantha and Sheryl are talking. Shortly after the lights come up, Sheryl's cell phone rings.

Scene VI

SHERYL: *(talking on her cell phone)* Hi. *(slight pause)* I don't believe it! Who's coming after him? *(slight pause)* They're not going to get him. Samantha, we've got a problem. Happy's video went viral and there're people who want to take him away.

Mom and Dad enter from stage right in the middle of Sheryl's phone conversation.

DAD: The story was just on the news. Some scientists want to take Happy to their lab and put him in a freezer. Somehow they figured out that Happy is by our house somewhere. They should be here within the hour.

MOM: Happy's a very special snowman. He's not some kind of wooly mammoth you just chop out of the ice and throw into a freezer.

SAMANTHA: Don't worry, Mom. I have a plan. They're never gonna get him. Come with me, Sheryl. We're gonna use our cell phones to organize a flash mob.*

SHERYL: What good will that do?

SAMANTHA: Remember last year when everyone showed up at the mall dressed like Santas? Well, we're gonna tell all our friends to dress up like a snowman and show up in our front yard.

Samantha and Sheryl exit stage right.

DAD: I get it. With a pile of people all dressed up like snowmen, the paparazzi and scientists will get confused. They won't know which one is Happy.

MOM: Yeah, the kids can surround Happy. Then they can lead him to a hidden spot where he can safely melt and return again to bring joy to another group of children.

Mom and Dad exit as the lights are turned off on the living room. Samantha and Sheryl appear on far stage right in the performance area. Callers are also on far stage left. As the kids make their calls, lighting is used to direct the audience's attention from one side of the performance area to the other. While the calls are being made or as soon as each call is finished, the children in the cast and some chorus members should be getting into their snowman outfits backstage and hidden from the audience. Spotlights come up on Sheryl at stage right and Randy at stage left.

SHERYL: Hi, Randy. There's no time to explain. We're organizing a flash mob for two o'clock in Samantha's front yard. Come dressed as a snowman and pass it on.

Spotlight off Sheryl, up on Katie at stage right.

RANDY: Hi, Katie. Flash mob in Samantha's front yard at two o'clock, dress as a snowman. Pass it on.

*"Flash crowd" or any other term of the teacher's choice may be substituted.

Spotlight off Randy, up on Kim at stage left.

KATIE: Kim, I need your help. There's no time to explain. We're holding a flash mob ... *(gets softer until inaudible)*

KIM: Sure, I'll be there.

Spotlights off Katie and Kim.

Scene VII

Lights come up on the outdoor scene as the three scientists, two news anchors, TV camera person, and paparazzi enter stage left. Happy is hiding behind the evergreen. The three scientists pantomime talking among themselves. The news anchors are standing at stage right of the outdoor scene with the camera person standing to the side taking the video.

NEWS ANCHOR #1:   With the aid of a weather satellite, the scientists have been able to hone in on the location of the snowman.

The scientists, with paparazzi in tow, are looking for Happy.

NEWS ANCHOR #2:   We suspect he's in this general area and will be found within the hour. Let's listen in on our three scientists and get a sense of what their strategy will be.

The camera person turns and begins to video the scientists who are now standing side by side. While the scientists are speaking, the paparazzi look for Happy.

DR. STORM: I've looked up the weather for today and the temperature is going to be well above freezing. We've got to get to that snowman before he melts. He needs to be frozen solid.

DR. MANKIND: The thought has crossed my mind, what if he's a relative of the Abominable Snowman? He might be dangerous! He could give us a very icy reception.

DR. FLOYD: That's true! Based upon my study of frigid psychosis ridiculosis, he might not be eager to cooperate.

While Dr. Floyd is speaking, Paparazzi #1 looks behind the evergreen and finds Happy. Song #6. ("Gotta Find Our Man Reprise") begins softly and is kept low enough for the lines to be heard.

6. GOTTA FIND OUR MAN! (REPRISE)

Scientists, Media, and Children

by MICHAEL and JILL GALLINA

Continuing the Tradition of Shawnee Press Excellence

HAPPY, THE HIGH-TECH SNOWMAN – Teacher Edition

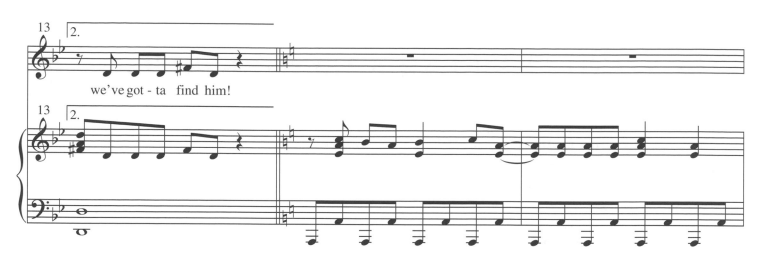

It's up to me and you___ to find him right now!___

We've got-ta find him right now!___

We've got-ta find him right now!___ We've got-ta find him right now!_

Right now!

PAPARAZZI #1:   I found him. He's here behind the evergreen.

PAPARAZZI #2:   He's not moving. It's the wrong snowman.

The paparazzi gather around Happy. As the flashes on their cameras start to go off, Happy is startled and comes out from behind the tree.

DR. STORM: No, that's him! Grab hold of him.

After Dr. Storm speaks, the flash mob of kids (dressed as snowmen) enter from all parts of the performance area and surround Happy. Happy gets mixed in with the flash mob and it exits stage left. The scientists and the paparazzi chase after them.

DR. FLOYD: Oh, no! Which one is the real snowman? Looks like a blizzard of walking, talking snowmen.

DR. MANKIND: The real one's wearing sunglasses.

DR. STORM: They're all wearing sunglasses!

When all have exited, Mom and Dad enter the outdoor scene stage right. Song #6. fades as the scene continues.

DAD: The scientists were only steps away from grabbing Happy. I wonder if the kids' plan will work.

MOM: *(sadly)* It's gotta work. Happy is a wonderful and gentle friend. I know if he can get away he'll return again. I'm so upset! I just don't know what to do.

As Mom is speaking, Samantha and her friends (still wearing their snowmen suits) enter stage left.

DAN: Mrs. Jones, your worries are over. Happy made a clean getaway.

SAMANTHA: Everything is fine. Come on, Mom. It's time to celebrate. Let's all get Happy!

7. GET HAPPY!

Cast and Chorus

by MICHAEL *and* JILL GALLINA

Continuing the Tradition of Shawnee Press Excellence

50

you'll get hap - py, that we guar - an - tee!

you'll get hap - py, that we guar - an - tee!

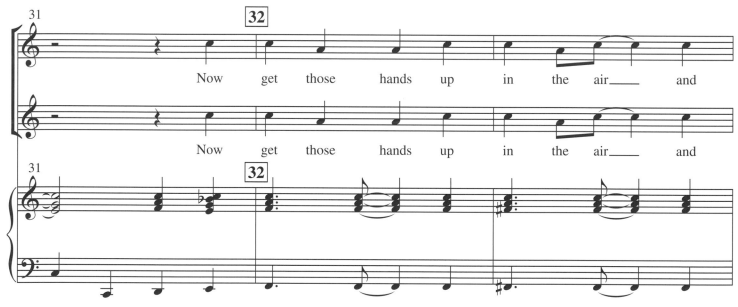

32

Now get those hands up in the air____ and

Now get those hands up in the air____ and

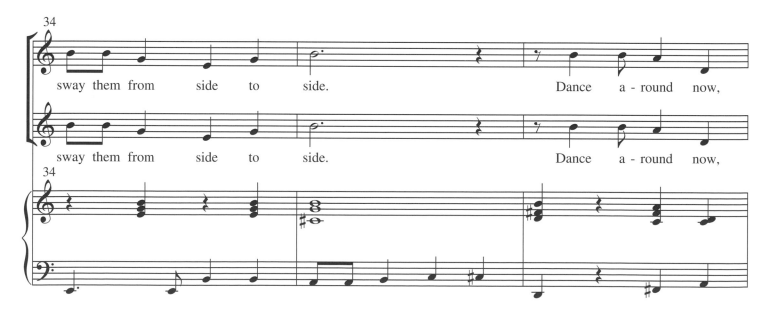

sway them from side to side. Dance a - round now,

sway them from side to side. Dance a - round now,

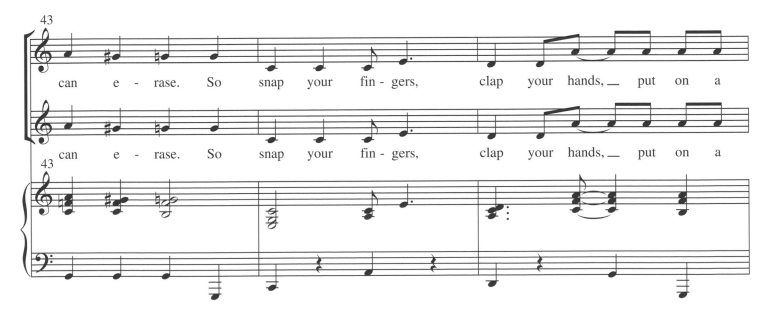

smile and soon you'll see ____ that you'll get hap - py.

smile and soon you'll see ____ And

and she'll get hap - py,

spoken

he'll get hap - py, Is ev - 'ry - bod - y hap - py?

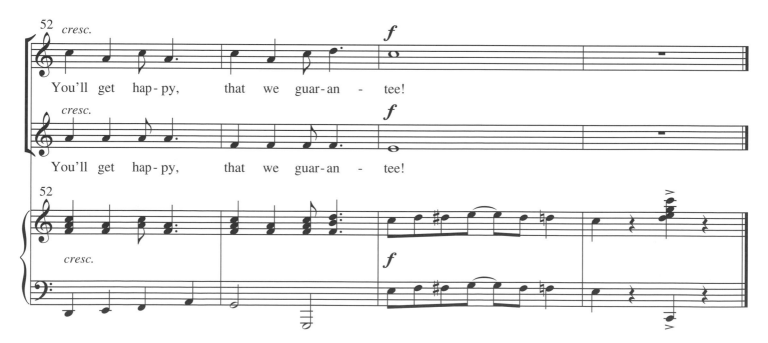

You'll get hap - py, that we guar-an - tee!

You'll get hap - py, that we guar-an - tee!

cresc. *f*

cresc. *f*

cresc. *f*

At the end of the song a cell phone text message chime is heard.

MIKE: Hang on a minute. I'm getting a text message. *(looks at his phone)* It's from Happy!

All kids ad lib. "What's it say?" "Read it to us." "Hurry up, read it." "Come on, read it!", etc.

MIKE: He says, "Made it back safe and sound. Will be back someday, and in the meantime ... *(reads slowly)* D-W-G-H."

All look puzzled and ad lib. "DWGH, what does that mean?" "Never heard of that." "That's a new one.", etc.

DAD: *(after a few seconds)* I've got it! I know what he means! *(speaks slowly)* D-W-G-H, don't worry ... get happy!

All cheer as song #7. "Get Happy" is reprised.

7. GET HAPPY! (REPRISE)

Michael and Jill Gallina have achieved national prominence as the country's foremost composers of musical plays and choral music for youth in elementary, middle, junior and senior high schools. Their clever creations in story and song have consistently won awards from the Parents Choice Foundation, American Library Service and ASCAP.

Their music has been featured on the Disney Channel, The World's Largest Concert, PBS, The Macy's Thanksgiving Day Parade and in a documentary on children's rights for the United Nations. In addition, the Gallina's are recipients of the Stanley Austin Alumni Award from the College of New Jersey for their many accomplishments in the field of composition.

Both Michael and Jill received B.A. degrees in music from the College of New Jersey. Jill was an elementary school music teacher before becoming a full-time composer. Michael completed a Masters degree in music from the College of New Jersey as well as a doctorate in administration and supervision from Rutgers University. In addition to his writing collaborations with Jill, he served as elementary principal of the Angelo L. Tomaso School in Warren, New Jersey and authored ***Making the Scene***, an illustrated "how-to" book for building sets, props and scenery, etc., for musical productions.

The Gallinas are inspiring teachers all across the English-speaking world with their music and educator workshops. Their chorals have sold millions of copies and their musical plays have thousands of performances across the globe each year. They are educating, enlightening, and engaging youth of today with their consummate talents and creativity